ADO   2

 **FOOTBALL**

FOOTBALL

by Ben Hodge, Sr.

A FIRST BOOK
FRANKLIN WATTS
NEW YORK LONDON 1977

Cover design by Ginger Giles
Diagrams by Rod Slater

Library of Congress Cataloging in Publication Data

Hodge, Ben.
    Football.

    (A First book)
    Includes index.
    SUMMARY: An introduction to the rules, equip-
ment, player's positions, scoring, and other aspects
of football.
    1. Football—Juvenile literature.   [1. Foot-
ball] I. Title.
GV950.7.H62   796.33'26'0973   75–6822
ISBN 0–531–00768–5

Contents

# Introduction

It's hard to say exactly when and where the modern game of football started. Some people feel it began as early as the eleventh century in England. They say that soldiers began kicking around skulls found on old battlefields.

In the twelfth century, people began playing with a ball. Sometimes hundreds of people would play at once. They would all rush after the ball and try to kick it to a certain place. Sometimes two towns would play. The people from one town would try to kick the ball to the center of the other town. The game was even rougher then than it is today. Many people were hurt during play. Some were hurt very badly. Some were even killed.

The game was not really football as it's played today. It may have been closer to the game of soccer. It was just a group of people kicking an object. There were no real rules, no positions. It was almost every man for himself.

A game very much like this was played in the early days of America. In fact, the Indians played it even before the white man came. But it was mainly a game of pushing and shoving, and sometimes fighting. There were no real rules for hundreds of years.

The ball was mostly kicked in these early games. No one really knows when the first man ran with the ball. The first time it was written down was in 1823 at the Rugby School in England. One player became very angry and suddenly picked the ball up and began running. Other players from both teams were surprised. They didn't know what to do. So everyone jumped on the runner. Even then, carrying the ball wasn't easy.

Soon others were running with the ball. By about 1839 it was part of the game played in England. It later became the English sport of Rugby, which is something between soccer and American football. Rugby is still played today.

The first college football game in America was played on November 6, 1869, between Rutgers and Princeton. Rutgers won, six goals to four. There were twenty-five players on each team. But the game was more like soccer than American football.

Slowly, but surely, the game began to change. In 1880, a man named Walter Camp lowered the number of players on a side to eleven. Camp was a student and later the first football coach at Yale University. He was also the first man to play with a line of scrimmage. That is, he had the players line up facing each other. Before that, they had all locked arms in a circle, as in Rugby.

Although each college and each team had its own rules, the game was slowly taking shape. The ball was sometimes tossed around in games. But the first real **forward pass** was supposed to have been used by Wesleyan University against Yale in 1906. It quickly became part of the college game and really became famous in 1913. That's when Knute Rockne (later a great coach at Notre Dame) and Gus Dorais used it for Notre Dame in an upset win over the great Army team. By 1912 a **touchdown** (or goal) was worth six points and a team had four **downs** (or tries) to gain ten yards. If they did it, they had another four downs to gain another ten yards. That's still the way the game is played today.

By 1920 both college and professional football were growing. Large crowds came to see the games. And by then the game of football was strictly an American sport. It was much the same as it is today.

Today, football is very close to baseball as the most popular sport in America. Thousands of fans across the country watch football games during the season. Those who can't go out to a stadium can see college and pro games on television.

Most high schools and colleges across the country have football teams. Many students come out to play the game every year. Pro football stars are national heroes. Young players everywhere go out hoping to be the next big star.

There are teams and leagues for all ages. Young people from nine to thirteen can play in Pop Warner leagues. As they get older, they can join school or club teams. By the time they reach high school, many young people love the game and want to play at the next level.

But it never gets easier. The players become better and practice more. And the game is rougher because the players are bigger and stronger. Football is still a very rough game. The players must be in very good physical shape. They can be hurt at any time.

Still, more young people are playing every year. And as a start, they must learn what the game of football is all about.

The Field, Equipment, and Officials

Football today is played with a definite set of rules. The players must use and wear the same kind of equipment. Games are watched by officials who make sure the players obey the rules. Once a person watches a few games, he finds that the rules are not that hard to learn.

Most high schools play under the same rules as the colleges. There are a few different rules in the pro game, but football today is pretty much the same game at each level. College rules are set up by the National Collegiate Athletic Association (NCAA), and the professional rules by the National Football League (NFL).

FIELD OF PLAY

The game is played on a level field which is 360 feet long and 160 feet wide. The field is sometimes called a **gridiron**. Most fields used to be covered with grass. Today some have an artificial surface much like a rug or carpet. Both kinds of fields are marked off with white lines according to the rules. The lines show where the field begins and ends. They also show where the ball is at the end of each play, and how far it has moved. Each line or set of lines has a name.

● **Sidelines** are marked along the length of the field on both sides. They show where the playing field ends. They separate the **in bounds** area from the **out of bounds** area.

● **End lines** run across the width of the field at each end and are connected to the sidelines to form a large rectangle.

● **Goal lines** are ten yards in from the end lines and also run across the width of the field. A team must move the ball across the goal line to score a touchdown.

● **Yardage lines** run across the field from sideline to sideline. There is a yardage line every five yards. They show where the ball is placed and how far a team must go for a first down and touchdown. In front of each goal line is the five-yard line, then the ten, fifteen, twenty, twenty-five, thirty, thirty-five, forty, forty-five, and fifty. The fifty-yard line marks the center of the field. The other side of the field is marked in the same way—leading up to the fifty-yard line in the center. Each team has its own goal and territory up to the fifty-yard line.

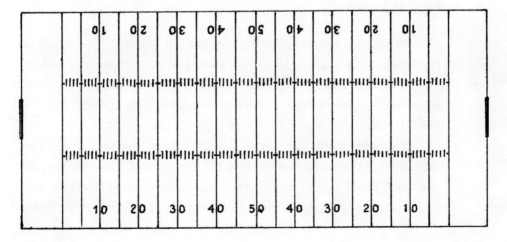

● **In-bounds lines** (also called hash marks) are short lines that run the entire length of the field. There are two sets. In college ball each set is fifty-three feet, four inches in from the sidelines. In pro ball they are seventy feet, nine inches in from the sidelines. In-bounds lines are marked across the yard lines. They are not connected. Each yard line has its own set of in-bounds lines. The in-bounds lines indicate where the ball is placed to start the next play. This happens only when the play stops outside them.

● **End zones** are the areas ten yards (thirty feet) deep between the goal lines and the end lines. There is an **end zone** at each end of the field. A touchdown is scored when the ball is brought into the end zone. It can be run across the goal line, or the ball can be caught in the end zone by a pass receiver on the scoring team.

There are also four short corner flags that mark the corners of the field where the sidelines meet the goal lines. And there is a three-yard line out from the goal line (a two-yard line in the pros). The ball is placed there when a team tries for an extra point or points.

When the ball crosses the sidelines it is out of bounds and play stops. On a pass play, a receiver can reach across the sideline to make a catch if his feet are still inside the line. In the pros, both the receiver's feet must be in bounds. In college ball, a catch is good if only one foot comes down in bounds.

The **goal posts** are set in the middle of the end lines. The crossbars of the posts are ten feet off the ground. The uprights on pro goal posts are eighteen feet, six inches apart. College uprights are twenty-three feet, four inches apart. When a team kicks for an extra point (after a touchdown) or for a field goal (worth three points), the ball must pass over the crossbar and between the uprights. Uprights must be at least thirty feet high in pro ball and twenty feet high in college ball. That makes it easier for the official to see whether a kick is good.

EQUIPMENT

There are several different parts to a football uniform. Pants are usually made of nylon or another strong cloth. The top, or jersey, is made of the same material. Shoes are generally made from leather and have **cleats** on the soles. The helmet must be very strong. It is padded inside and there is a face guard to protect the mouth, nose, and eyes. There is also a chinstrap to help hold it on during collisions on the field.

Players must also wear padding for more protection. There are shoulder pads that go under the jersey. Kidney pads fit around the hips and are covered by both pants and jersey. The pants are also padded at the knees and thighs. If a player has had an injury, he may wear a special pad or brace to help him protect the injured part of his body.

Opposing teams must wear different-colored jerseys so that the fans and officials can tell them apart. Jerseys usually have numbers on the front and back. Today, many college teams and most pro teams have the players' names on the back above the numbers.

The Ball

The football is oval-shaped, like a thin, pointed egg. It is 11 to 11.25 inches long, and 6.85 inches in width in the middle. The outside is usually made of four pieces of leather. Inside there is a rubber bag, which is blown up with air. When blown up correctly, the football weighs fourteen to fifteen ounces. The football is sometimes called a "pigskin."

OFFICIALS

College games usually have five officials. Professional games have six. The officials are there to see that the game is played by the rules. Each official has a title and a special job to do.

● **The referee** controls the game. He is the man who whistles the play dead. He is responsible for placing the ball before the next play. He handles any problems the teams have. He gives the signals for all fouls and marks off the yardage for the penalties. He also makes the final decision on the interpretation of any rules. He is the chief official.

● **The umpire** makes sure the players have the right equipment. He also watches for violations on the line of scrimmage (attack).

● **The linesman** or **head linesman** has a big job. He must watch for offside or encroachment violations at the line of scrimmage. He assists the referee in determining the forward progress of the ball carrier. He must also tell when and where a ball or player has gone out of bounds. The linesman also controls the down marker and yardage chain. The down marker shows which down is to be played and just where play begins on that down. The yardage chain shows how much ground is needed for a first down. The yardage chain is ten yards long with each end attached to a pole. When there is a first down, it is placed even with the ball and then stretched ten yards ahead. This is

(9)

OFFICIAL SIGNALS

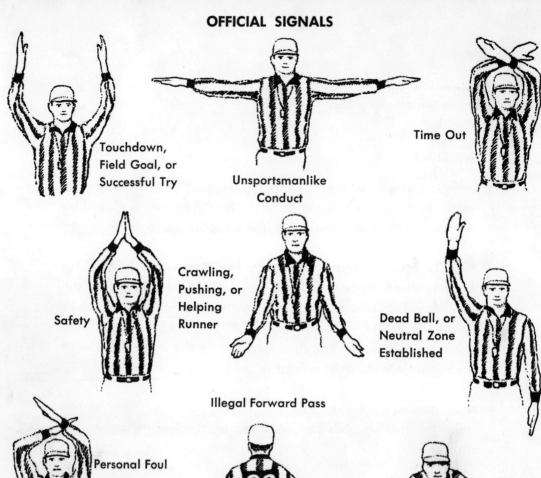

Touchdown, Field Goal, or Successful Try

Unsportsmanlike Conduct

Time Out

Safety

Crawling, Pushing, or Helping Runner

Dead Ball, or Neutral Zone Established

Illegal Forward Pass

Personal Foul

Same signal followed by swinging leg: Running into or Roughing Kicker

Same signal followed by raised arm swinging forward: Running into Passer

Same signal followed by hooking one foot behind the opposite ankle: Tripping

Same signal followed by hand striking back of calf: Clipping Below Waist

Same signal followed by hand striking back of thigh: Clipping Above Waist

Illegal Cut

Same signal followed by raised hand flung downward: Intentional Grounding of Pass.

First Down

Loss of Down

Ineligible Receiver,
or Ineligible Member
Of Kicking Team
Downfield

Offside,
Encroaching,
or Free Kick
Violation

Illegal Motion
At Snap

Invalid
Fair Catch
Signal

Holding

Illegal Use
of Hands

No Time Out,
or Time In
With Whistle

Interference With
Forward Pass,
or Fair Catch

Penalty Refused,
Incomplete Pass,
Play Over, or
Missed Goal

where the ball must go for another first down. In pro ball there is a second linesman called a **line judge** who stands on the side of the field opposite the linesman. In addition to helping the linesman watch for offside violations, he keeps time of the game as a backup for the clock operator. He has the primary responsibility of determining whether a passer is behind the line of scrimmage when he throws a forward pass.

● **The back judge** stands in the defensive backfield. He watches for violations on pass plays and running plays that come into his area.

● **The field judge's** position is even farther down field than that of the back judge and on the same side as the head linesman. In addition to watching for violations in his area, he is the man who keeps track of the time between plays to make certain that the offense does not exceed the thirty second rule. He also times the intermission periods and time outs.

All officials use a handkerchief (called a **flag**) to signal a foul or violation. If an official sees a violation, he throws the flag at the point of the foul. Then, when the play ends, the officials make the call and step off any penalty there might be.

How Football Is Played

There are many different rules in football. Yet the game is not really hard to learn. Once the basics are learned, the rest comes easy.

There are, of course, two teams. Each team has a head coach. He is the boss, the man in charge of everything. Most teams have one or more other coaches. Pro teams have a coach for each position. All the coaches work together to train and teach the players. They also make up the **game plan** before the team takes the field. The game plan tells a team the best way to attack the other team's defense and stop their offense.

The object of the game is to score points. There are several ways to do this. A touchdown, worth six points, is scored by a player running the ball over the other team's goal line, or catching a pass in the end zone between the goal line and the end line. A **field goal,** worth three points, is made by kicking the ball over the crossbar and between the uprights on the opponents' goalpost. A **safety,** worth two points, occurs when the runner or passer is trapped in his own end zone. The offensive team tries to score points, while the defensive team tries to stop the other team from scoring.

There are four quarters in a game. In college and professional games, each lasts for fifteen minutes, so the actual playing time of the game is one hour. Of course, with time-outs, and the clock stopping on other occasions, plus half time and time between quarters, a football game can take almost three hours to complete. High school games do not take as long because the quarters are twelve minutes each.

Before a game begins, the officials and the team captains meet in the middle of the field. The captains are picked by the coach or team members. There can be a single captain or several, called cocaptains. They are on the field for the **toss.** The referee flips a coin into the air and asks the captain of the visiting team to call heads or tails. (The home team is the one playing on their own field.) The captain who wins the toss has a choice. He can decide to have his team begin the game by kicking or receiving the ball. Or he can choose which goal his team wants to defend in the first quarter. The captain who lost the toss then makes the other choice. In other words, if the winning captain decides to receive the kick, the losing captain decides which goal to defend.

At the beginning of the second half, the captain who lost the coin toss has first choice of kicking or receiving, or choice of goals. At the end of the first and third quarters, the teams always change goals. That way, the same team isn't going in one direction the whole game. There may be an advantage to moving a certain way on the field. Either the sun or wind might make it harder to move the ball. So the teams switch goals to make things even.

The game itself begins with the **kickoff.** The ball is kicked from the kickoff team's forty-yard line in high school and college, and the thirty-five-yard line in the pros. The line is sometimes called the **restraining line.** No player on the kickoff team may go past the restraining line until the ball is kicked. Players on the receiving team must stay ten yards from the ball until it is kicked. This is their restraining line.

There are also kickoffs at the beginning of the second half, and after each touchdown or field goal.

For the kickoff, the ball is generally placed on a **holder** or **tee.** The ball stands upright on the tee until it is kicked. Sometimes a player will hold the ball. He stands it almost straight up and places his finger on the top. He releases his finger at the same moment the kicker's foot hits the ball.

The referee's whistle starts the game. When it blows, the kicker runs toward the ball. The other ten players begin moving, too. But they are slightly behind the kicker. As soon as the ball is kicked, the players charge downfield at full speed.

The ball must go at least ten yards or be touched by a member of the receiving team for the kickoff to count. Once it goes ten yards, it's a **free ball.** Anyone on either team can grab it.

A number of different things can happen on a kickoff:

1) Most kickoffs are usually caught far downfield by a member of the receiving team. He then runs the ball as far as he can toward the opponents' goal line. This is called the return or **runback.** Sometimes the kickoff is very high and the kicker's

teammates get downfield quickly. The return man knows he will not have a chance to make a good return. He will be hit too quickly. He may even fumble. So he can signal for a **fair catch** by raising one hand in the air. This means no man may tackle him and he cannot run the ball back. But he must still catch it. If he drops it, it's a free ball.

2) Sometimes the ball is kicked over the receiving team's goal line and into the end zone. A player receiving the ball in the end zone may do one of two things. He may try to make a regular runback. Or he may drop down on one knee after he gets the ball. This means he does not want to return the ball. This is called a **touchback**. It means no one may tackle him. The ball is then brought out to the twenty-yard line, and the receiving team has a first down from there.

3) If the kickoff goes over both the goal line and end line, it is an automatic touchback. There cannot be a runback and the ball is again given to the receiving team on their twenty-yard line.

4) Another type of kickoff is called the **onsides kick**. A kicking team generally tries an onsides kick when it's losing the game with time running out. The onsides kick is a very short kick. The ball is placed on its side and kicked along the ground so it will be difficult to catch. Once the ball goes ten yards or is touched by a member of the receiving team, the kicking team can try to get it. So the team making the onsides kick is trying to recover the ball so it will be in a fairly good position to score. If the receiving team recovers the onsides kick, they are in a good field position. That makes the onsides kick a gamble. But it is sometimes a necessary one.

Once the kickoff has been completed the regular play from

(16)

scrimmage begins. The team that has the ball is called the offense or offensive team. The opposing team is the defense or defensive team.

The offensive team will try to move the ball by running or passing. The defensive players will try to stop the offense by grabbing the ball-carrier and throwing him to the ground. This is called tackling or making a tackle. When there is a pass, the defensive team will try to tackle the player before he throws, or knock the pass down. They can also try to catch the pass themselves. This is an **interception** and would give them the ball and make them the offensive team.

When a player is running with the ball, his teammates try to help by running ahead of him, beside him, and even behind him. This is called running interference. Today, it is mainly known as **blocking,** since that is what the players are trying to do. Blocking is done by the offensive players throwing their bodies in front of or against the defensive players. Blockers cannot use their hands to stop a defensive player. Use of hands is illegal. It is a personal foul and carries a fifteen-yard penalty. In pro ball the penalty is ten yards if the foul occurs at or behind the line of scrimmage. It is also illegal to block a man from behind. This is called **clipping.** Clipping also carries a fifteen-yard penalty from the point of the foul. So players must learn the right way to block, just as they must learn the right way to tackle. It takes a great deal of practice to become good at these things.

Each attempt by the offense to advance the ball is called a down. The offense has four downs or tries to advance the ball ten yards. When the offense makes ten yards within four downs, they have earned another first down. The offense then has four

more tries to make another ten yards. When a team is moving the ball well and making a number of first downs, it is called a **drive.** If they score a touchdown, it's called a touchdown drive.

   If the offense does not gain at least ten yards in four downs, it loses the ball. The other team gets the ball at the point the last play ended. Then they become the offensive team with a first down going the other way. There are other ways that a team may give up the ball, such as punting. This will be described later.

In professional football, and in most colleges and a good number of large high schools, coaches have complete offensive and defensive units. The offensive unit plays when the team has the ball. The defensive unit comes on when the other team has the ball. This is called **two-platoon football.**

In the old days, the same players stayed in the game on both offense and defense. That made the game even harder. But there were new rules that allowed free substitution. Coaches could then substitute as many players as they wanted, whenever they wanted to. They found it was better to have an offensive unit and a defensive unit. That way, a player could train for one position and work to become really good at it. And he wouldn't have to be on the field as long. He could rest more and play his position even better. So in today's game, from high school right to the pros, two-platoon football is used whenever possible.

As mentioned earlier, college and pro games are divided into four, fifteen-minute quarters. Between the second and third quarters (or first and second halves) is a long time-out called **half time.** It is usually fifteen to twenty minutes long. Teams can rest and plan for the second half. The fans are usually entertained by a marching band and other things. Between the first and second, and third and fourth periods there are just one minute time-outs (two minutes in pro ball). This is just long enough for the teams to change goals and get set up again.

The clock is stopped by the referee for the following reasons during the course of the game: (1) when a score is made; (2) when a touchback or automatic touchback is made; (3) when a pass is incomplete; (4) when the ball goes out of bounds; (5) when it is necessary to discuss a play, or move the ball during a penalty, or because of an injured player; (6) after a change of possession. These are called official time-outs.

Each team may stop the clock three times during a half. These are time-outs and last for one and a-half minutes (two minutes in pro ball). Teams use time-outs to rest, make plans, and to keep the other team from running out the clock.

After a time-out and between plays, a team must start its next play within a set amount of time. In high school and college, teams have twenty-five seconds to get the next play off. In the pros they have thirty seconds. If a team doesn't start its next play in that time, a **delay-of-game** penalty is called, and the team loses five yards.

The Players

OFFENSE

There are eleven players on an offensive football team. They are divided into two groups, the line and the backfield.

   The offensive line must have at least seven players. They are usually the center, two guards, two tackles, and two ends. Before each play, these players line up just behind an imaginary line that runs across the back end of the football. This is called the line of scrimmage.

   On a balanced line (Formation 1), the man in the middle is

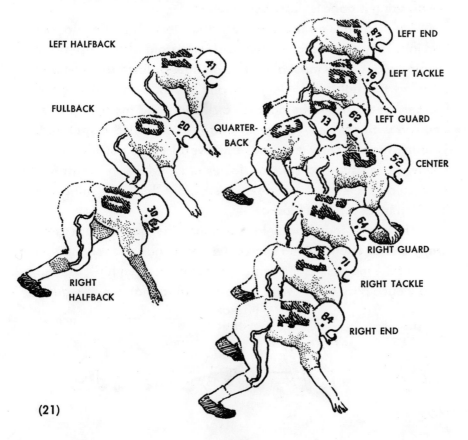

the center. He is bent over with his hands on the ball. The right guard is the player to the right of the center. Next to him is the right tackle and then the right end. On the left side of the center are the left guard, left tackle, and left end.

The center, guards, and tackles are called **interior linemen.** They are always big and strong. In the pros, an interior lineman might weigh 240 to 300 pounds. Their main job is to block. The center starts each play by passing the ball between his legs to the quarterback. This is called the snap. After that, all five interior linemen follow the blocking plan for that play. It is blocking that makes a good interior line. The two main blocking jobs are blocking for the runner and blocking for the passer. The way the blocking is done is described later.

The two ends on the line must also block. They have a second job. They must catch passes. But on certain plays, especially running plays, they must block like an interior lineman. One end is called the **tight end.** He is usually a big man and a good blocker. He must also be able to catch short and medium passes and run with the ball. The other end is often called a **split end.** That means he sometimes lines up several yards outside of the tackle. He is usually a smaller, faster man, who can run downfield quickly to catch long, deep passes. But there are still plays in which he becomes a blocker.

There are four backfield positions. The quarterback generally stands right behind the center. He bends over slightly so he can take the ball as the center passes it between his legs. This is how each play starts. With some special formations, the quar-

SPLIT
END

INTERIOR
LINEMEN

TIGHT
END

terback might stand several yards behind the center. The play still begins with the center pass, only it is a little longer.

The quarterback also calls the signals. He tells his teammates what kind of play to run. The quarterback must be a good all-around player. He must be able to run and pass. In the pros, it is very important that the quarterback be an outstanding passer.

There are three other players in the backfield. In the old days they were usually called the right halfback, left halfback, and fullback. The halfbacks were quick, fast runners who lined up a step or two behind the quarterback and to the right and left of him. The fullback, usually a bigger man and not so fast, was deeper in the backfield and directly behind the quarterback.

In today's game there are many different formations. The quarterback remains the same, but the other backs are frequently just called running backs. Most teams still use a big back to run inside through the line, and one or two smaller backs to go outside around the ends. In the pros, there are usually just two running backs behind the quarterback. The third back serves as a pass receiver. He is called the **flanker** back. Sometimes he splits out of the backfield. That means he stands five or ten yards to the right or left and a yard behind the line of scrimmage. Other times he lines up in the slot between the tackle and split end. But he is still part of the backfield.

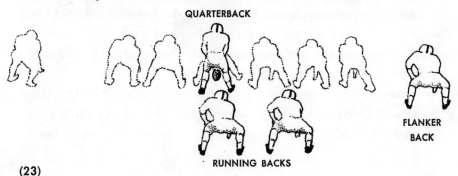

QUARTERBACK

RUNNING BACKS

FLANKER BACK

DEFENSE

The defensive team also has eleven players on the unit. There are many different formations for defenses today. The defensive line can have any number of players on it, but usually has from three to seven men on it. It depends on the game and the offense. The defensive linemen line up directly opposite the offensive linemen. They get as close to the nose of the ball as they can without going over the line of scrimmage. The defensive linemen must try to stop the other team's running game. They also try to tackle the quarterback before he can pass. This is called a **pass rush.**

There are many different names for defensive linemen. They are usually just defensive tackles and defensive ends. But sometimes defensive linemen are called nose guards, middle guards, and various other things. Most pro teams use four defensive linemen. They are called the **front four** and consist of two tackles and two ends. Pro linemen usually weigh from 240 to 300 pounds.

Just behind the defensive linemen are two, three, or four players called linebackers. They play a very important position. Linebackers often come right up to the line and rush the passer. Or they must jump in and try to tackle the ball-carrier. Sometimes they must move quickly to the outside to stop a player running around the end. And they must be fast enough to cover a backfield man going out for a pass. So linebackers must not only be big and tough, they must be fast and agile as well. Linebackers usually weigh from 215 to 240 pounds in the pros. Most college players are somewhat lighter.

Behind the linemen and linebackers comes the defensive backfield. Once again there are many ways to set up the defensive backfield. Sometimes there are three men back there, sometimes four, sometimes even five. They are usually smaller, faster men who are very quick on their feet. They must stop fast ball-carriers in the open field. And they must defend against all kinds of passes, from short to very long ones. And since pass receivers are very fast, the defensive back must be fast also. They usually weigh from 175 to 210 pounds in the pros.

Pro football teams usually have four defensive backs. The two outside backs, who play to the outside and slightly behind the linebackers, are called cornerbacks. Behind them, toward the middle of the field, are the safetymen. They are the last defenders. Some college teams use one safetyman. Others use a player as a rover back or **monster man**. He is usually an outstanding football player. The coaches let him play wherever he feels he will be needed most in the defensive formation. He must decide where the play will be and try to stop it. The monster man can come up near the line or play at safety. He is free to choose.

Defensive formations can be quickly written by adding the number of players in each line of defense, starting with the line. For example, a 6-2-2-1 defense would mean there were six men on the line, two linebackers, two cornerbacks, and one safety. The pro defense is usually a 4-3-2-2 line-up, but some teams will change that in certain situations.

SAFETYMAN

CORNERBACKS

LINEBACKERS

DEFENSIVE LINEMEN

 **The Game**

After the kickoff (if it has not been returned for a touchdown), the offensive team begins to run its plays, or series. Members of the offensive team begin by forming a **huddle.** The eleven players form a circle so that the quarterback can announce the next play. Most times the quarterback has the job of calling the play. He decides what will work best. Some coaches like to call the plays from the sideline. They do that by sending a substitute player into the game. He joins the huddle and tells the quarterback what play the coach wants to call. (Coaches sometimes call the play by signaling from the sidelines.)

Sometimes the plays have a number. Sometimes they have a short code name. That way, the play can be called quickly. No one has to explain to each player what his job is. Every team has a **playbook** that describes each play in detail as well as the job of each of the players.

The offensive team then breaks the huddle and comes to the line. They line up in whatever formation the play calls for. Of course, they must have at least a seven-man line. The defensive team can then line up in the best formation for stopping the offense. That's why defensive players are often jumping around the line at the last instant.

The offensive linemen usually get down in a **three-point stance.** This means they are bent over with both feet and one hand planted on the ground. This stance allows a player to move quickly in any direction. At the same time it keeps the defense from knowing what that direction will be before the ball is snapped. The quarterback stands behind the center, knees bent, hands just under the center's rump. The running backs are usually in a three-point stance also. Sometimes the wide receivers (split end and flanker back) will stand upright, perhaps with their hands on their hips, ready to move quickly.

Usually, defensive linemen are also in a three- or four-point stance (both hands on the ground). The linebackers and defensive backs stand up, perhaps crouching slightly.

Between the offensive line and defensive line is a small **neutral zone.** It is at least as wide as the length of the football. Only the offensive center (leaning over the ball) can have any part of his body in the neutral zone when the ball is snapped. Anyone else in the neutral zone when the ball is put in play is **offside.** That brings a five-yard penalty. Occasionally an over-anxious defensive player will move into the neutral zone before the snap. If he does not make contact with an opposing player and manages to return to his side of the zone before the ball is snapped, there is no penalty. If a player moves into the neutral zone and makes contact before the ball is snapped, he is guilty of encroachment. This is also a five-yard penalty.

After both teams are lined up, the quarterback **calls the signals.** That means he shouts a series of numbers or sounds (sometimes just "hut, hut, hut") that the whole offense can hear. Each member knows the signal at which the ball will be snapped. That way they can all move at once and the play begins.

FORMATIONS

There are many formations that an offensive team can use to begin a play. Each formation is planned for a certain kind of play or plays. The following formations are used very often.

(27)

T-formation

The straight-T is one of the oldest formations in the game. It's called the T-formation because the four backfield men form the letter T. The straight-T is mainly a running formation. The four

STRAIGHT-T

backfield men are all fairly close together so they can try to fake or draw the defensive men out of position. When the ball is snapped, the whole backfield starts to move. The quarterback can then pretend to hand off to the right halfback. The right halfback also pretends he has the ball and runs straight into the line. If the fake is good, some of the defensive linemen will go after him. The quarterback, however, still has the ball. Now he can give it to his left halfback. If the fake worked, the left half-back will have more running room.

The T formation is not always used with a balanced line. It can also be used with an unbalanced line. This is when the tackle from the left side of the line is shifted to the right side. He is be-tween the tackle and the guard. This formation favors plays to the strong side (the side with more linemen), but the offense can still run plays to the other side, or weak side, to try to catch the defense napping.

STRAIGHT-T (UNBALANCED LINE)

Two slight changes from the straight-T are the split-T and the tight-T. In the split-T the line is split. There is a small space between the center and guard. Then there is a larger space between the guard and tackle, and a still larger space between the

SPLIT-T

tackle and end. The line in the tight-T is generally closer together. There are no spaces because everyone is as tight in to the center as they can be. From a split-T formation the quarterback is likely to call a play for one of his runners to go wide. In the tight-T he

TIGHT-T

(29)

is likely to take advantage of the blockers in front of him. He can either pass or send a runner up the middle.

There are still other ways the basic T-formation can be used. One of these is the winged-T. That is when one of the running backs moves closer to the line and to the outside of the

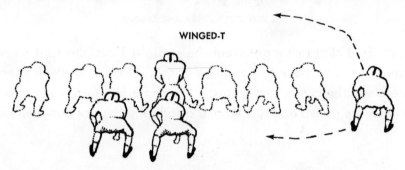

WINGED-T

end. He then becomes a wingback and can either run out for a pass or cut back into the backfield to carry the ball.

The **wishbone-T** (or Y-formation) is the latest type of T. It is basically a running formation. It must have a quick, talented quarterback and a strong, speedy fullback. In the wishbone-T the quarterback is behind the center as usual. But it is the full-

WISHBONE-T

back who is close behind the quarterback. The halfbacks are behind and to either side of the fullback. Notice how the back-field looks like a wishbone or Y.

(30)

In the wishbone, the quarterback has three choices. That is known as a **triple option.** He can give the ball to his fullback, who can run into the line in any one of several different ways. Or the quarterback can pitch out to either halfback, who will try to run wide. He can also keep the ball himself and begin running. If there is a hole, he can keep going. But if not, he can pitch the ball back to the halfback. The quarterback then becomes a blocker out in front of his halfback.

A quarterback can also drop back and pass from the wishbone. Yet it is mainly a college formation. Pro coaches don't like it because they don't want their quarterbacks running and blocking that much. A pro quarterback is too important to his team. In the wishbone, there is a greater chance that a quarterback might be injured.

The veer is a tactic used in the wishbone-T offense and in many combinations form a variety of formations. A back quickly veers from one point of attack to another through or around the line. It is often used by the University of Houston and called the Houston Veer.

Double Wingback Formation

Notice the positions of the players in this formation. Look at the backfield men on the far right and left. The double wingback formation provides a balanced attack for running or passing on either side.

DOUBLE WINGBACK

I-formation

A team can have both a running and passing attack from this formation. The running attack is very strong inside the tackle because of the extra blocking from the fullback. The deep back, or **tailback,** is usually the main runner from this formation. Many colleges use it, and some pro teams are beginning to line up in the I part of the time.

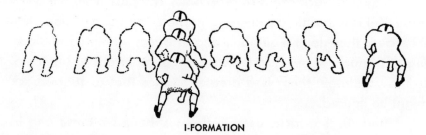

I-FORMATION

Shot Gun Formation

In this formation the quarterback stands about ten yards behind the center. He is the deepest man in the backfield. This is usually a passing formation. The quarterback can take a direct snap from the center and be ready to pass. His running backs are lined up in front of him and can either block or run out as pass receivers.

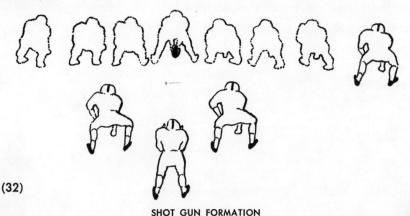

(32)

SHOT GUN FORMATION

Motion and Shift Formations

There are several types of plays in which one or more players can move before the ball is snapped. Teams use these motion or shift plays to confuse the defense, but there are strict rules that must be obeyed.

When the offensive team comes out of the huddle and goes into formation, the players must remain completely stationary for at least one full second before the ball is snapped. If they don't, they can be penalized five yards for being illegally in motion.

However, after a full second, one offensive player may start moving even if the ball has not yet been snapped. But he can only move backward or sideways, not forward. This is called a man in motion.

MAN IN MOTION

For example, the flanker back will sometimes go into motion and move through the backfield to the other side before the ball is snapped. This puts him on the other side of the field when the play starts. The quarterback then hopes he will be free to catch a pass.

A **shift** occurs when two or more players change position

before the snap. They do this by waiting a full second after assuming a set position. Then they move to their new positions. Then the team must wait at least another second before the snap.

THE PLAYS

There are just three ways to advance the ball. They are running, passing, and kicking. Kicks are used only in special situations. Running and passing plays make up most of a team's offense.

There are basically four types of running plays. They are line plunges, off-tackle plays, trap plays, and end runs.

Line Plunge

In the line plunge, the running back usually drives straight ahead through the line. He runs right over the center or guard positions. The guard and center must try to open a hole for the runner. They do this by blocking or shoving the defensive players aside. The runner tries to get through the hole as quickly as he can. Defensive players must plug the hole and try to make the tackle.

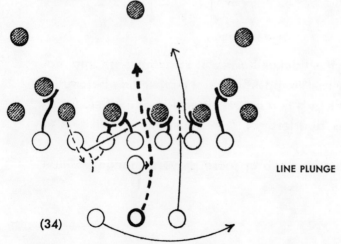

LINE PLUNGE

(34)

Other offensive players must also block on the play. If the runner gets through the hole into the secondary (beyond the line of scrimmage), he needs more help. So either the tackles, ends, or perhaps another running back must move into the secondary. That way they can try to block linebackers and defensive backs. On each running play everyone has a job to do. Blocking assignments are known before the play begins. Therefore each player knows which defensive player he must try to block. The line plunge is generally used to gain short yardage, anywhere from one yard on up. If the blocking is perfect and the running back is quick, he can sometimes "break one" and gain big yardage.

Off-Tackle Play

In this play, the runner heads for the line just outside the tackle position. The play is like the line plunge, but through a different spot in the line. The linemen still try to open a hole for the runner by blocking. The difference is that a runner can gain bigger yardage on the off-tackle play. If he gets through the hole he can cut to the outside where there are fewer players. But for just short yardage, there is a better chance to make it

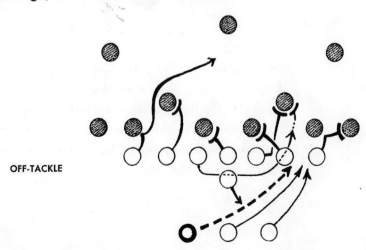

OFF-TACKLE

with a line plunge. That's because the runner can hit quicker. He can get into the line faster than on the off-tackle play.

Trap Plays

This play needs a great deal of practice to run. The timing must be perfect for it to work. At the snap, one or two offensive linemen—perhaps a tackle and guard—do not block one of the de-

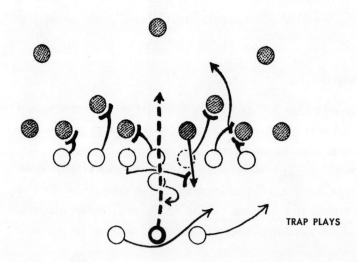

TRAP PLAYS

fensive linemen. They let him charge straight in. But once he breaks through, they then block him. They are trapping him, hoping to let the runner slip through the hole that the trapped player has left in the defensive line. The runner must also wait a second before making his move. This gives the linemen a chance to work the trap.

End Runs

End runs are just what they sound like. The runner carries the ball around either the right or left end. He usually has several blockers in front of him. Sometimes the guard and tackle, or both guards, will **pull.** This means that at the snap they break to the side on which the play is going. They may be joined by the other running back. The three then go around the end in front of the ball-carrier. They try to cut down the defenders by block-

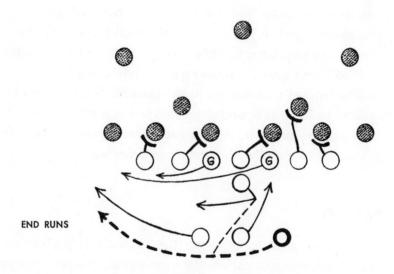

END RUNS

ing them. If this play works, the runner can gain big yardage. But if the blocking breaks down, a defensive player can come through and tackle the runner for a "loss." This means he is tackled behind the line of scrimmage, before he can get around the end. The play takes a great deal of practice and good timing. End runs are also called **sweeps** or power sweeps.

(37)

FUMBLES

If a running back drops the ball during a play, or has it pulled or pushed from his grasp, it is a **fumble**. Anyone can recover it because it is a free ball. If the runner or another member of the offensive team recovers it, play continues from that point. If a defensive player recovers the fumble, play stops. His team then takes over the ball at that point. They now go on offense with a first down.

There are other ways fumbles can happen. The quarterback can drop the snap from center. Or the ball can get loose when the quarterback is giving it to the ball-carrier. In the pros, a player can pick up a fumble and run with it. In high school and college it can only be recovered. A player can't run with it unless he catches it before it hits the ground. If a fumbled ball rolls or is kicked out of bounds, the ball belongs to the team that last had possession of it. If it is recovered after the ball hits the ground, only the offensive team can advance it.

PASSING

The second way to advance the football is by passing. The really good teams, especially in the pros, usually mix running and passing plays. This helps to confuse the defense. They can't guess what is going to happen. There are certain times when a team must pass more than it runs. That's because it is easier to gain big amounts of yardage if passes can be completed. But there is also more of a chance of losing the ball through an interception. That's when a player on the defensive team catches the ball.

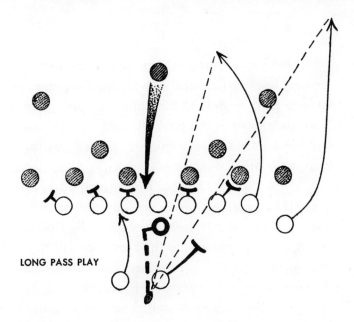

LONG PASS PLAY

The long pass, or long **bomb,** is one of the most exciting plays in football. The defense works very hard to stop it. It takes a quarterback with a very strong arm to complete a long pass. He must also have good protective blocking from his linemen, and very fast pass receivers to run out and catch the ball.

The basic pass play works like this. As the quarterback takes the snap from center everyone begins moving. The quarterback may fake to a running back or just **drop back** to pass. This means he takes the snap and quickly retreats seven or eight yards behind the line of scrimmage. The interior linemen don't fire ahead to block, as with running plays. They just try to hold their ground and keep the defensive linemen and maybe linebackers from coming in. The defenders try to get to the quarterback before he can pass. This is called a pass rush. Sometimes a safetyman will suddenly rush up to the line and try to get the quarterback. This is called a safety blitz.

While this is happening, one or two ends, and perhaps a running back, will break downfield. They are running **pass patterns** or pass routes. This means they will go to a specific area. Since defensive backs and linebackers are covering them, they will have to move very quickly. Sometimes they fake one way and go the other way.

While the quarterback is dropping back, he looks downfield to see if his receivers are in position and open (free to receive). If one is open, the quarterback throws the ball over the heads of the opposing players to his receiver. If the man downfield catches the ball, the quarterback has completed a forward pass. If he drops the ball or cannot reach it, the pass is "incomplete."

Only the two ends and three running backs can receive a forward pass. If any of the interior linemen catch the ball, the offensive team loses the down and is penalized fifteen yards (ten yards in pro ball). Quarterbacks like more than one man running pass patterns so that they can pick the best one to throw to. Naturally, the quarterback must be behind the line of scrimmage when he throws the ball.

On an incomplete pass, the ball is brought back to the line of scrimmage and the offensive team has used up a down. If an incomplete pass is thrown on the fourth down, the ball goes over to the other team at the original line of scrimmage. If the passer cannot find an open receiver and is tackled by a defender, the ball remains at the point where the tackle was made, and the team loses both yardage and a down. This is called "sacking the quarterback," or just a **sack.** If the quarterback thinks he is going to be sacked and throws the ball to the ground, a penalty is called. The offensive team loses the down and is penalized five yards in college and fifteen in the pros for "intentionally grounding the ball." If the quarterback begins running around the backfield to get away from the pass rushing defenders, he is **scrambling.** He can keep running for yardage or throw the ball before he reaches the line of scrimmage.

If a pass is intercepted by a defender, that player is allowed to run as far as he can toward his opponents' goal line before he is tackled or forced out of bounds. His team then takes over with a first down. Any member of the defensive team can make an interception.

There are many different types of pass plays and pass formations. Pro teams generally pass more than college teams because they all have very good passers. In recent years, college teams have been passing more, perhaps because the quarterbacks have been practicing from an earlier age.

Pro defenses are always trying new ways to stop the pass. In the 1960s, many pro teams were throwing long bombs. At that time, the defenses were using man-to-man coverage. That meant that each receiver had just one defender on him. Very fast receivers could often get free deep downfield.

Today's defenses have learned to stop the bomb better than ever. Many use a zone defense. That means that each defender covers a particular area of the field, or zone, rather than a particular man. That way, the defenders can help each other more and stop the deep receivers from getting free.

With new defensive formations, the pro teams now try to draw the defenses in. They do this by throwing short passes. Many teams like to throw short passes to the running backs instead of the ends. But when a team is behind and has very little time to score, it will often throw long to try to get points quickly.

If a quarterback throws the ball to a player behind him rather than in front of him, it is called a backward or **lateral pass.** But it is not really a pass. For if a lateral is dropped, it is a fumble and not an incomplete pass. That means the defensive team can recover the ball.

THE PUNTING GAME

If by the fourth down a team has not gained ten yards, it has to make a decision. The team can use the fourth down to try to make the ten yards for a first down. But if it doesn't make it, the other team gets the ball. If the offensive team is deep in its own territory, trying for a first down is taking a big chance. But the offensive team can put the other team in a poorer field position by **punting.** This is using the fourth down to kick the ball to the other team.

In punt formation, the kicker stands about twelve to fifteen yards behind the line of scrimmage. Most punters take two steps

before kicking, so he has to be far enough back to have the time to get the kick away. His teammates will block for him in the same way they block for the passer. They will try to keep the defenders out long enough for him to punt. The punter takes a long snap from center. Then he steps forward and drops the ball in front of him. He kicks it before it hits the ground.

A good punter will try to kick high and deep most times. Once he kicks the ball, his teammates stop blocking and race downfield. The defensive team usually has one or two players waiting to receive the punt. The man catching the punt may try to run it back the same way a kickoff is run back. If he feels he doesn't have a chance to make a runback, he can raise his hand and signal for a fair catch. This means he cannot be tackled, but he cannot run it back either. His team gets the ball at the spot he catches it. If he drops the ball, it is a fumble, and either team may recover it.

If a punt goes into the end zone, the receiver may run it out. Or he may down it for a touchback. Then it comes out to the twenty-yard line. If the punt goes behind the end zone, it is an automatic touchback and comes out to the twenty. If the punt goes out of bounds before reaching the end zone, the receiving team has a first down at the spot where the ball has gone out. Some punters try to kick the ball out of bounds inside the twenty-yard line. This prevents a runback and also a touchback. A punter who kicks for the out-of-bounds line between the ten-yard line and goal line is said to be kicking for the **coffin corner**. Of course, when a punt goes out of bounds, the ball is brought out to the **hash marks** before play resumes.

The defensive team may also block the punt. If they block it, they get the ball at the point where it is recovered, no matter which team recovers it. However, any player from either team who picks up a blocked punt may run with it. If a defensive player slams into the punter without blocking the kick, there is a "roughing the kicker" penalty called. The defenders' team is penalized fifteen yards. This means the punting team will have the ball again. Many times the penalty gives them a first down. (In pro ball there is a penalty called "running into the kicker" and it carries a penalty of five yards and an automatic first down.) So trying to block a punt can be quite a gamble.

There is one other thing a punter can do. He can fake a punt and either run with the ball or pass it. This is taking a big chance. For if he doesn't make a first down, the defensive team will get the ball in good field position. Teams do not use the fake punt very often.

TRICK PLAYS

The fake punt is an example of a trick play. There are various other trick plays an offense may use during a game. Most teams have these plays in their playbooks. But they do not use them very often. One trick running play is the **reverse**. In this play, the

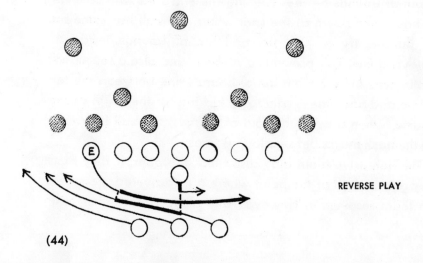

REVERSE PLAY

quarterback will give the ball to a halfback who begins running around, say, the left side of the line. At the same time the left end breaks to the right, and when he passes the runner, he is given the ball. The direction of the play is then "reversed" as the end runs around the right side of the line. A team using a reverse hopes to catch the defenders going the wrong way. If it works, it can be a big gainer. But if it doesn't, it can result in a big loss.

There are also trick passing plays. One is called the **flea flicker.** On this play, the quarterback gives the ball to a runner who begins running around the end. Suddenly the runner stops and passes the ball back to the quarterback. (Both must be behind the line of scrimmage.) The quarterback will then throw a forward pass to a receiver downfield. A team using the flea flicker hopes the pass defenders will have run up to stop the ball-carrier. This would leave the receiver open downfield. But this is also a hard play to make work and is not used very often.

There are other trick plays that you will see from time to time. They are always exciting to watch. But coaches usually like to stay with the basic running and passing plays.

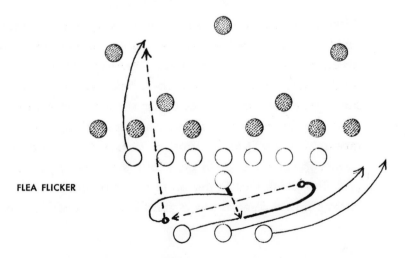

FLEA FLICKER

 **Scoring**

As with most other games, a football game is won by the team scoring the most points. Points can be scored in the following ways.

TOUCHDOWN

A touchdown is scored whenever any part of the ball is on, above, or behind the opponents' goal line, and the offensive team is in legal possession of it. The ball may be run over the goal line on either a running or passing play. A pass may also be caught in the end zone for a touchdown. A recovered fumble in the opponents' end zone also counts as a touchdown, whether the fumble is made by the offensive or defensive team. A touchdown always counts six points.

POINT(S) AFTER TOUCHDOWN

After scoring a touchdown, a team is given a chance to score another point or points. This is known as the extra point, point after, or conversion. A team can score the extra point in one of three ways. They can kick the ball between the uprights, run the ball across the goal line, or complete a forward pass across the goal line. In the pros a team can score only one extra point, no matter whether it kicks, runs, or passes for it. In college, a kick counts one point, a run or pass counts two extra points.

The place kick is the most common method of scoring the extra point. If a team has a good kicker, he will make the extra point almost every time. Of course, he must have blocking or a defender can come in and block the kick. Running or passing for the point is more of a gamble. Pro teams always kick, because they can only get the one point. College teams will usually kick. Only if they feel they need the two points to win the game will they try a run or pass. They may also try it if they do not have a good kicker. But today most college teams have kickers good enough to make the extra point. In the pros, the ball is placed on the two-yard line for the conversion. In college ball it is placed on the three-yard line.

To kick for the extra point, the ball is snapped by the center to a "holder." He is about seven yards behind the line of scrimmage and down on one knee. He must catch it, then quickly place it on the ground in an upright position. He balances the ball by holding the top with his finger. At the same time the kicker takes two quick steps forward and kicks the ball a split second after it is placed down. It takes a great deal of practice between holder and kicker, but a good kicker rarely misses this short kick.

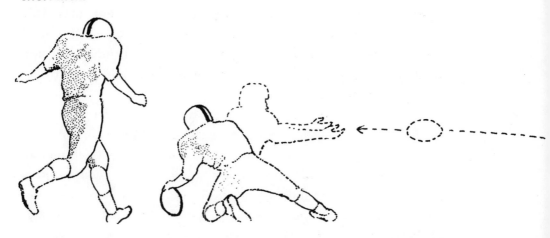

The defensive team rush and try to block the kick. If they do, the point is no good. But if they run into the kicker and foul him, the team gets another chance. In the run or pass, the defensive team tries to stop the offense the same way they would from any scrimmage play. Many games have been won or lost on the extra point try. It is very important.

FIELD GOAL

A field goal is scored by the offensive team when the ball is kicked through the opponents' uprights. It counts three points. A team can try a field goal any time it chooses from anywhere on the field. But there are only certain times and from certain places when it is a good football move.

A team will usually try for a field goal when it feels it is close enough for its kicker to reach the goal posts. At the same time the team must feel it doesn't have much of a chance to score a touchdown on its drive. For instance, if a team is on its opponents' twenty-yard line, and it is fourth down with nine yards to go for a first down, they may try the field goal. The odds are that they would not make the first down on the next play. Then they would lose the ball. So if a touchdown is not badly needed at that time, the team will try the field goal. Three points are better than none.

Almost all pro and college teams have one player who kicks the field goals. He usually kicks off and kicks the extra point, too. He is a kicking specialist. Sometimes that's the only thing he does. There are two kinds of kickers today. The old style is when the kicker comes straight at the ball and kicks it with his toe. The new style is to come from the side and kick it with the instep of the foot, swinging the leg across the body. This is a soccer-style kick. Many ex-soccer players are now kicking for football teams using this style. Most pro and many college kickers can make a thirty-yard field goal most of the time. The farther out from the goal they are, the harder it is. But some kickers have made field goals from beyond the fifty-yard line.

If a field goal is missed, but the ball crosses the goal line it is a touchback. In colleges, the ball comes out to the twenty-yard line, and the other team takes over. In the pros, the ball comes out to the twenty or to the place where it was kicked if the place is farther than the twenty. So if a field goal is missed and the line of scrimmage was the thirty-three-yard line, the ball comes out to there. If the line of scrimmage was the fifteen, then the ball comes out to the twenty.

A missed field goal that falls short and does not go out of the end zone can be run back just like a kickoff or punt. And as with other kicks, the defensive players can try to block a field goal. The same rules regarding roughing the kicker apply here as in punting, so the defenders must be careful. Field goals have become a big part of both pro and college games. Very few games go by without one or more field goals being tried.

SAFETY

A safety counts two points. A safety is scored when the player with the ball is tackled behind his *own* goal line. It usually happens when a team is deep in its own area, usually inside the ten-yard line. Sometimes the quarterback drops back into the end zone to pass and is tackled there before he can throw. Sometimes a runner tries an end run and goes into his end zone before turning the corner. If he's tackled in the end zone, it's a safety.

After a safety, the offensive team has one play to get rid of the ball. They have a free kick from the twenty-yard line. They may either punt or kick off to the other team. Teams don't usually want a safety. It gives the other team two points as well as the ball. As a result, safeties do not happen very often.

In a rare case, a team might deliberately make a safety. This would be to stop the other team from taking over the ball behind the goal. The team would forfeit two points instead of six as a touchdown.

Training and Conditioning

Football is a very rough game. The hitting is very hard. Players cannot let up at all or someone will run right over them. It is very important for all football players, from the Pee Wee Leagues right to the pros to be in the best possible physical condition. They must also be ready for the special skills needed to play a certain position.

A football player must have stamina. He must be able to play a game without getting tired. A tired player can get hurt more easily than a fresh one. Thus it is important for a football player to do a great deal of running. Running builds up the legs and also builds stamina. Running backs, pass receivers, defensive backs, and even linebackers must do a great deal of running during a game; they should be ready for it. A pass receiver might be asked to go long (deep into the opponents' territory) on three straight plays without the ball being thrown to him once. If he gets tired, he won't be ready when the ball *is* thrown.

Runners must also be ready to give a fast burst of speed at any time. Thus it is important for them to practice their **wind sprints.** That means running very hard for ten or fifteen yards, stopping for a second, then running hard for another ten or fifteen yards. They must do this over and over again so they can "turn it on" when they have to during a game.

It is also important for runners, pass receivers, and defensive backs to be able to change direction quickly. So they should also practice their **cutting.** That means changing direction as quickly as possible. The quicker a man can cut, the better he will be on the field.

The legs are very important to all football players. Besides running, many players make their legs stronger by working with weights. There are special machines for this purpose. Most good football programs will have them available. Interior linemen must be especially strong in the legs. They need this strength for blocking, holding their ground, and rushing the passer.

Defensive linemen and linebackers must also be very strong in the arms and shoulders. They will need their strength to make tackles and get through blocks. They, too, often work with weights and with special equipment to become as strong as they can.

Quarterbacks must be strong and quick, and they must practice their throwing. That means they must work to make their throwing arms stronger. And they must also be able to put the ball where they want it. Many practice by trying to throw a football through a swinging tire.

Pass receivers must also work on their catching. If a receiver has great legs, can cut well, and run all day, it still won't help if he can't catch. So receivers must practice. Their fingers should be spread and should give slightly when the ball hits their hands. This is often called having **soft hands.** They let the ball just settle in their hands. If they don't do this, the ball may bounce out before they can grab it.

So training and physical condition are most important to all football players. It's necessary for players of all ages to practice and train hard. But they must also get the right amount of rest and eat the right foods. Every little thing counts. Almost all the really good players know how to take care of themselves. If they don't, they can get hurt. Or their careers may be cut short. It is one of the first things any football player must learn.

 # Penalties

The following is a list of some common penalties that might be called during a football game. Watch for them.

1) Fifteen-Yard Penalties:

Roughing the kicker. (Automatic first down in pro ball.)
Roughing the passer. (Automatic first down.)
Unsportsmanlike conduct.
Clipping.
Offensive holding.
Offensive pass interference. (plus loss of down) (In pro ball it is a ten-yard penalty.)
Intentional grounding of forward pass. (plus loss of down)
Ineligible receiver downfield. (In pro ball it is a ten-yard penalty.)
Unnecessary roughness.
Defensive holding. (In pro ball it is a five-yard penalty.)

2) Five-yard penalties:

Offsides.
Delay of game.
Illegal formation.
Illegal motion.
Illegal shift.
Illegal substitution.
Running into the kicker.
Too many time-outs.
Too many men on the field.

(53)

Post-Season Games and Awards

Both the college and professional football scenes stay busy after the regular season ends. College football gets busy picking its All-America teams. These are the best players from schools all over the country. Newspapermen, announcers, and coaches all have a chance to pick All-America teams.

There are also awards for the best players. The most well-known is the Heisman Trophy, which goes to the best college player in the land. It is usually won by a quarterback or running back from a top school. That's because a player at one of those positions is in the limelight. There is also an award for the best lineman. It is called the Outland Trophy and is important for the future of the player who wins it. But the Heisman is still the big prize.

College football also has postseason bowl games. These are games that match some of the best teams in the country. The big bowl games are the Rose Bowl, Orange Bowl, Sugar Bowl, and Cotton Bowl. They are played on New Year's Day. There are now many other lesser bowl games, some matching fine teams, too. They take place during most of the holiday season. There are also all-star games, such as the Blue-Grey, and East-West games. They have the best players from a certain section of the country against the best players from another section.

Pro football is busy with its playoff schedule. The top four teams from the National and American Conferences begin a series of postseason games. First there is a semifinal in each conference. Then the remaining teams play for the conference championships. And finally the two teams that are left play for the pro championship. That game is called the Super Bowl and is watched by millions and millions of fans all over the country.

The pros also have a kind of All-America team. Only it's called the All-Pro Team and is made up of the best players on both offense and defense. A Player of the Year is also named for each pro conference. This is like a most valuable player award. And finally the top players from each conference meet in the last football game of the season, the Pro Bowl. It's played near the end of January and the long football season is finally at an end. It begins again the following July when the pro players report to training camps.

 # Glossary

The following is a list of common football terms. Some have been mentioned in the text. Others have not. But the football fan and player will come across all of them as he follows and plays the game.

Backfield in motion: A violation calling for a five-yard penalty. It occurs when one or more members of the offensive backfield move forward before the ball is snapped.

Balanced line: An offensive line in which the center is in the middle, with a guard and tackle on each side of him. If two guards or two tackles are on the same side, it becomes an unbalanced line.

Blitz: An all-out charge by any number of defensive backs and/or linebackers to rush the passer with the hope of catching the offense by surprise. (Also called red dogging or shooting the gap.)

Blocking: The act of slowing or stopping an opponent's progress by shoving him or knocking him down.

Bomb: A very long pass play made in the hope of completing it for a big gain or touchdown.

Cleats: Raised round object on the sole of the football shoe that allows the player to get better footing on the field.

Clipping: A foul that occurs when a blocker hits or pushes a man from behind. It calls for a fifteen-yard penalty.

Coffin corner: The sideline area very near the goal line where punters often try to kick the ball out of bounds. This will give the receiving team poor field position and not allow a runback.

Cutting: Term used to describe a sharp turn or change of direction made by a runner trying to escape a tackler.

Deep receiver: A pass receiver going way downfield for a long pass.

Delay of game: A violation called when a team does not get a play off within thirty seconds. The result is a five-yard penalty.

Double coverage: Two players defending against a single offensive player, usually a pass receiver or runner.

Down: A single play by the team with the ball. It begins with the snap from center and ends when the play is completed.

Drive: Name given to a series of plays in which the offensive team advances the ball toward the opponents' goal line.

Drop back: The quick retreat some seven yards or so by the quarterback when he is preparing to throw a forward pass. He usually drops back into the pocket.

End zone: The area between the goal lines and end lines on each end of the field. The end zone is ten yards deep; a touchdown is scored when the ball is run into it or a pass caught in it.

Fair catch: The catch of a kick by a receiver who does not want to run it back or be tackled. He must signal this by raising his arm above his head as the ball is coming down.

Field goal: A scoring play in which the offensive team kicks the ball over the crossbar and between the uprights of the goal post. It is worth three points.

Flag: Name given to the rag thrown on the ground by the officials when they have detected a violation of the rules.

Flanker: A member of the offensive backfield who splits out wide to the left or right, and whose primary job is pass receiver.

Flea flicker: Trick pass play in which the quarterback hands off to a runner, who then passes back to the quarterback. The quarterback then looks downfield for an open receiver.

Forward pass: A ball thrown to a receiver in the direction of the opponents' goal line.

Foul: A violation of any playing rule.

Free ball: Any ball in play that is loose and can be recovered by either team. When a ball is fumbled, it is a free ball.

Free kick: A kickoff or kick after safety. It is a kick that cannot be blocked by the defense.

Front four: A four-man defensive line made up of two tackles and two ends.

Fumble: The loss of the football during a live play by the player in possession.

Game plan: An overall play by which an offense plans to attack a defense or a defense plans to stop an offense.

Goal posts: Structures set on the middle of the end lines. Each goal post has a crossbar ten feet off the ground and uprights a set distance apart. Extra point kicks and field goal tries must pass over the crossbar and between the uprights to be good.

Gridiron: A nickname given to the entire football field.

Half time: A rest period between the second and third quarters during which the teams can plan for the second half of the game.

Hand-off: The exchange of the football between the quarterback and one of his running backs.

Hash marks: Short lines drawn across each yardage line on both sides of the field and a specific distance in from the sidelines. They show the officials where to place a ball after a play has ended outside the hash marks.

Holder: Name given to the player who holds the football for extra point and field goal tries. The holder must balance the ball perfectly in a split second so the kicker can meet it just right.

Holding: A foul occurring when an offensive player uses his hands to slow down or stop a defensive player. Defensive linemen can use their hands to ward off an offensive blocker. However, defensive holding is called when a defender uses his hands to stop a pass receiver from running his pattern. Holding carries a fifteen-yard penalty.

Huddle: A circle of offensive or defensive players before a play begins. The purpose is for the quarterback or defensive captain to give the other players instructions about the upcoming play.

Illegal motion: Can be the same as backfield in motion. Also covers the offensive interior linemen who cannot move or take their hands off the ground before the ball is snapped. Results in a five-yard penalty.

Interception: The act of a defensive player catching a forward pass thrown by an offensive player. An interception results in the ball going over to the intercepting team.

Interior linemen: General name of the five offensive linemen who play between the ends. They consist of the center, two guards, and two tackles.

Kickoff: A free kick that opens each half and is also used after a touchdown and field goal.

Lateral: A pass that is thrown sideways or backwards from the line of scrimmage.

Man-to-man coverage: A pass defense where defenders cover specific receivers rather than an area of the field.

Monster man: A roving defensive player who has a choice of lining up wherever he feels the play will be. Usually used in college defenses. (Also called rover back.)

Neutral zone: The area between the offensive and defensive lines before the snap.

Officials: The men who make sure the game is played by the rules. There are five officials in high school and six in college ball, and the pros.

Offside: A violation occurring when either an offensive or defensive lineman charges into the neutral zone or past the line of scrimmage before the ball is snapped. Results in a five-yard penalty. Also called if a player on the kickoff team or receiving team passes his restraining line ahead of the kickoff.

Onsides kick: A short kickoff along the ground that the kicking team hopes to recover before the defensive team can. An onsides kick not touched by a member of the receiving team must go at least ten yards to be in play. If it doesn't go ten yards, a five-yard penalty is called.

Option play: A play in which the quarterback has the choice of running with the ball, handing it off, or passing.

Pass interference: A foul in which a player prevents an opponent from catching a forward pass by pushing him, holding him, or knocking him down. If the violation is by the defensive team the penalty is a first down at the point of the foul.

Pass patterns: Term used to describe the way a receiver runs out for a pass. He usually knows just where he will go before the play starts. The quarterback knows too. Also called pass routes.

Pass rush: The attempt by defensive players to tackle the quarterback before he can throw the ball.

Place kick: The act of kicking off or trying for a field goal when the ball is held upright on the ground or sits upright on a kicking tee.

Playbook: A large book that lists all of a team's plays and the job that each player must do on those plays.

Pocket: An area of protection for a passer that is formed by his blockers.

Pulling guard: Term to describe a play in which a guard does not block straight ahead, but instead pulls out of the line at the snap and leads a runner around the end.

Pulling guard or tackle: An offensive lineman who pulls out of the interior line and runs to the right or left to provide blocking for an end run or sweep.

Punt: A kick made when the ball is dropped from the hands of the punter and kicked before it touches the ground.

Restraining line: A name given to the point at which the ball is kicked off, usually the forty-yard line. No player on the kicking team can cross the restraining line before the kicker's toe meets the ball. The restraining line for the receiving team is a line ten yards in advance of the kicking team's restraining line.

Reverse: A running play in which a runner starts in one direction then hands the ball to a second runner (usually an end) moving in the opposite direction.

Roll out: The act of the quarterback running to his left or right before throwing or keeping the ball himself.

Runback: The return of a kickoff, punt, or missed field goal by a member of the defensive team.

Sack: The tackling of the quarterback before he has a chance to throw the football.

Safety: A scoring play in which a player is tackled behind his own goal line and in his own end zone. The other team gets two points.

Scrambling: Term used mostly in pro ball to describe a quarterback who is running around the backfield to escape tacklers while trying to find an open pass receiver.

Scrimmage line: An imaginary line running through the point of the ball nearest a team's own goal line.

Shift: Change of positions at the same time by two or more offensive players after the play is ready to start, but before the ball is snapped.

Slotback: A back in between the wide receiver and nearest interior lineman. He must be one yard behind the line of scrimmage.

Snap: The passing of the ball between the center's legs to the quarterback, punter, or holder for a place kick.

Soft hands: Term to describe the way in which a pass receiver lets the ball settle into his hands.

Split end: A pass receiver split away from the tackle on either the right or left side of the line.

Sudden death: A pro rule only in which an extra period is started when a game ends in a tie. The first team to score in any way (touchdown, field goal, safety) wins the game. If neither team scores during the sudden death period, the game ends in a tie. In the playoffs and championship game, there are as many sudden death periods as needed to determine a winner.

Sweep: A running play in which the ball-carrier runs around either the right or left side of the line, led by one or more linemen.

Tailback: The deepest running back in a formation where the runners line up one behind the other.

Tee: A small device used to hold the ball straight up on kickoffs.

Three-point stance: A starting stance used by many linemen and running backs in which the player bends over and balances himself on just one arm. Thus his arm and two feet on the ground form the three points of the stance.

Tight end: An offensive end who lines up on the interior line next to the tackle. He can either block or go out for a pass.

Time-out: A short stop of play called by one of the teams or by the officials.

Toss: The toss of the coin before the game to determine how the game will begin, who will kick and who will defend a certain goal.

Touchback: A ball that is downed by a player in the end zone. It can be called by a kick returner or a player making an interception who chooses not to run the ball out. The ball is automatically brought to the twenty-yard line. A ball passing through the end zone on a kick is an automatic touchback and also comes out to the twenty.

Touchdown: Name given to a score worth six points. A touchdown is scored when a team advances the ball over the goal line into the end zone.

Trap block: A play where the defender is allowed to penetrate the line only to be blocked from the side, or trapped, by another lineman or back.

Triple option: Term used for a quarterback who has a choice of running the ball, passing it, or handing it off to a running back.

Two-platoon football: Term used when there is a separate offensive unit and separate defensive unit on the same team. Most college and pro teams today play two-platoon football.

Wide receiver: A general name given to a split end or flanker back who is set wide of the scrimmage line.

Wind sprints: A training exercise in which a player will run for ten or fifteen yards as hard as he can, stop for a second or two, then run hard again.

Zone defense: A pass defense in which the defenders cover specific areas of the field rather than specific pass receivers. It is the opposite of man-to-man coverage.

Index